THE PRAYER THAT WORKS

"Therefore I say unto you, What things soever ye desire, when ye pray, believe that ye receive them, and ye shall have them."

Mark11:24

By
Franklin N. Abazie

The Prayer That Works

COPYRIGHT 2018 BY Franklin N Abazie
ISBN: 978-1-945-133-69-5

All right reserved. This book or any portion thereof may not be reproduced or used in any manner whatsoever without the express written permission of the publisher, except for the use of brief quotations in a book review. All Bible quotes are from King James Version and others as noted.

Published by: F N ABAZIE PUBLISHING HOUSE---
a.k.a,
Empowerment Bookstore:

That I may publish with the voice of thanksgiving and tell of all thy wondrous works. **Psalms26:7**

To order additional copies, wholesales or booking: Call the Church office (973-372-7518)
or Empowerment Bookstore Hotline 973-393-8518
Worship address:
343 Sanford Avenue Newark New Jersey 07106
Administrative Head Office address:
33 Schley Street Newark New Jersey 07112
Email:pastorfranknto@yahoo.com
Website www.fnabaziehealingministries.org
Publishing House: www.fnabaziepublishinghouse.org

This book is a production of F N Abazie Publishing House.

A publication Arms of Miracle of God Ministries 2018
First Edition

CONTENTS

THE MANDATE OF THE COMMISSION...........iv

ARMS OF THE COMMISSION............................v

INTRODUCTION...viii

CHAPTER 1

1. What are Keys to Effective Prayer Life? 25

CHAPTER 2

2. What are Hindrances to Prayer?........................43

CHAPTER 3

3. Prayer of Salvation..81

CHAPTER 4

4. About the Author...89

THE MANDATE OF THE COMMISSION

"THE MOMENT IS DUE TO IMPACT YOUR WORLD THROUGH THE REVIVAL OF THE HEALING & MIRACLE MINISTRY OF JESUS CHRIST OF NAZARETH.

I AM SENDING YOU TO RESTORE HEALTH UNTO THEE AND I WILL HEAL THEE OF THY WOUNDS, SAID THE LORD OF HOST."

ARMS OF THE COMMISSION

1) F N Abazie Ministries-Miracle of God Ministries (Miracle Chapel Intl)

2) F N Abazie TV Ministries: Global Television Ministry Outreach.

3) F N Abazie Radio Ministries: Radio Broadcasting Outreach.

4) F N Abazie Publishing House: Book Publication.

5) F N Abazie Bible School: also called Word of Healing Bible School (W.O.H.B.S)

6) F N Abazie Evangelistic Ass: Miracle of God Ministries: Global Crusade

7) Empowerment Bookstore: Book distribution.

8) F N Abazie Helping Hands: Meeting the help of the needy world wide

9) F N Abazie Disaster Recovery Mission: Global Disaster Recovery.

10) F N Abazie Prison Ministry: Prison Ministry for all convicts "Second chance"

Some of our ministry arms are waiting the appointed time to commence

FAVOR CONFESSION

Father thank you for making me righteous and accepted through the blood of Jesus Christ. Because of that, I am blessed and highly favored by God. I am the subject of your affection. Your favor surrounds me as a shield, and the first thing that people see around me is your favored shield.

Thank you that I have favor with you and man today. All day long people go out of their way to bless me and help me. I have favor with everyone that I deal with today. Doors that were once closed are now opened for me. I receive preferential treatment, and I have special privileges, I am Gods favored child.

No good thing will he withhold from me. Because of Gods favor my enemies cannot triumph over my life. I have supernatural increase and promotion. I declare restoration to everything that the devil has stolen from my life. I have honor in the midst of my adversaries and an increase in assets, especially in real estate and expansion of

Because I am highly favored by God, I experience great victories, supernatural turnarounds, and miraculous breakthrough in the midst of great impossibilities. I receive recognition, prominence, and honor. Petitions are granted to me even by ungodly authorities. Policies, rules, regulations, and laws are changed and reverse on my behalf.

I win battles that I don't even have to fight, because God fights them for me. This is the day, the set time and the designated moment for me to experience the free favor of God, that profusely and lavishly abound on my behalf in Jesus name. **Amen**.

INTRODUCTION

"And he spake a parable unto them to this end, that men ought always to pray, and not to faint." **Luke18:1**

One of the greatest secret of the kingdom of God is the mystery behind answered prayer. *"Call unto me, and I will answer thee, and show thee great and mighty things, which thou knowest not."* **Jer33:3**

This book is to encourage every saint of God to pray. As long as there is a man to pray, there is a God to answer. *"O thou that hearest prayer, unto thee shall all flesh come."* **Psalm65:2**

Unless you travail in prayer, you will not prevail with answers. Therefore prayer is a form of spiritual labor.

"Epaphras, who is one of you, a servant of Christ, saluteth you, always labouring fervently for you in prayers that ye may stand perfect and complete in all the will of God." **Colossian4:12**.

The truth is *prayer works*, but we must know the master keys to make it work. In my opinion this book on prayer will help you make the best of your *spiritual life*.

I believe *this manual is of great help to anyone who is determine to make prayer a lifestyle*. I plead with you to neglect my phonetics and grammar but pay attention to the context of the text as revealed by the Holy Spirit.

Happy Reading!

HIS DESTINY WAS THE CROSS….

HIS PURPOSE WAS LOVE…..

HIS REASON WAS YOU….

"But thou, when thou prayest, enter into thy closet, and when thou hast shut thy door, pray to thy Father which is in secret; and thy Father which seeth in secret shall reward thee openly."

Mathew6:7

Encounter Prayer Points

"If ye shall ask any thing in my name, I will do it.." **John 14:14**

Holy Spirit of God frustrate and disappoint, every one that is against my life and family, in the name of Jesus.

Father Lord destroy every demonic networks and traps against my progress in life in the name of Jesus.

Fire of God, destroy every demonic projection and curses against my life and destiny in the name of Jesus.

Every spell and curses pronounced against my destiny, break, in the name of Jesus.

Hand of God cage every power militating against my rising in life, in the name of Jesus.

Power of God silent every voice raising a counter motion against my elevation,

Blood of Jesus neutralize every spirit of Balaam hired to hinder my life, ministry, and career, the name of Jesus.

Fire of God destroy every curse that I have brought into my life through ignorance and disobedience, break by fire, in the name of Jesus.

Ancient of day destroy every power harassing my ministry in the name of Jesus.

Father God deliver me from invincible forces militating against my life and destiny.

Power of God frustrate every coven and demonic network, designed to frustrate and hinder my success in life, in the name of Jesus.

I dismantle every strong hold designed to imprison my talent in the mighty name of Jesus.

I reject every cycle of frustration, in the name of Jesus.

Power of God paralyze every agent assigned to frustrate my life in the name of Jesus.

Finger of God, grant me supernatural speed against all my contenders in the name of Jesus.

By the blood of Jesus, I destroy every familiar spirit caging my life and career.

Fire of God arrest every demonic agents, assigned to police my destiny and marriage.

By the blood of Jesus, I proclaim no weapon fashioned against me shall ever prosper.

Holy Spirit of God break me through and forward in life in the mighty name of Jesus.

God, smash me and renew my strength, in the name of Jesus.

Holy Spirit, open my eyes to see beyond the visible to the invisible, in the name of Jesus.

Father Lord grant me strength and power in the name of Jesus

O Lord, liberate my spirit to follow the leading of the Holy Spirit.

Holy Spirit, teach me to pray through problems instead of praying about, it in the name of Jesus.

Father Lord, deliver me from the false accusation in life, in the name of Jesus

By the blood of Jesus, every evil spiritual padlock and evil chain hindering my success, be roasted, in the name of Jesus.

By the blood of Jesus I rebuke every spirit of spiritual deafness and blindness in my life, in the name of Jesus.

Father Lord, empower me to dominate the enemy of my destiny in the name of Jesus.

Jesus Christ of Nazareth, heal my infirmities in the name of Jesus

Lord, anoint my eyes and my ears that they may see and hear wondrous things from heaven.

Father Lord, anoint me with power and authority to dominate all my enemies in the name of Jesus.

Fire of God roast every giant rising up against my life and career.

Holy Spirit of God destroy all my oppressors in the name of Jesus.

Angels of good new, bring my good news to me in the mighty name of Jesus.

Every strong man holding me down, lose your hold now in the name of Jesus.

I nullify every demonic prediction over my life in the name of Jesus.

By the blood of Jesus, I flush out every polluted deposit of the enemy in my life.

By the blood of Jesus, I paralyze every enemy of my promotion in the name of Jesus.

Father Lord, destroy any power tormenting my life that is not from you.

Holy Ghost fire, ignite the fire of revival in my life.

By the blood of Jesus, I declare victory over every conflicting trial

By the Blood of Jesus, I command the arrest of every demonic spirit, militating against my life

By the blood of Jesus, I proclaimed the blood of Jesus, over every device of the enemy.

By the blood of Jesus, I revoke stagnation and hardship over my life in the name of Jesus.

Holy Ghost fire, destroy every satanic arrangement in my life, in the name of Jesus.

WHY DON'T WE PRAY?

For the most part, most people will tell you that they do not pray because they do not get result or have the time to pray. Although a few others have their personal reasons, in my opinion, there is no reason that will justify prayerlessness. According to the bible *"prayerlessness is a sin."*

It is written, *"Moreover as for me, God forbid that I should sin against the Lord in ceasing to pray for you: but I will teach you the good and the right way."* **(1samuel12:23)**.

Although Jesus commanded us to *"pray without ceasing"* studies have suggested that an average Christian spends less than ten minutes per day in prayer. Below is a few reasons why Christians don't pray.

~We Don't Believe

Unbelief is a stigma that will prevent anyone from praying to God. As long as you do not believe in prayer, unbelief will prevail, it will stop any precious saint from connected genuinely to God.

It is written, *"Jesus said unto him, If thou canst believe, all things are possible to him that believeth."* **(Mark 9:23)**.

We must develop the right mind-set. It is written, *"... for he that cometh to God must believe that he is, and that he is a rewarder of them that diligently seek him."* **(Hebrews 11:6)**.

For unless we let this mystery settle in our heart, unbelief will always hinder us from praying to God. If we don't come to Him in prayer we eventually don't believe. When doubt, and unbelief settles in our heart God will not answer our prayers.

Apostle Paul said *"How then shall they call on Him in whom they have not believed"* **(Romans 10:14)**. Only fools doubt the power of prayer. The truth is, unbelief will disadvantage anyone of us from praying, and from obtaining the promise.

It is written, *"Call unto me, and I will answer thee, and show thee great and mighty things, which thou knowest not."* **(Jer 33:3)**. Smith Wiglesworth believe that if you pray once for healing –that's faith, but if you pray repeatedly that is unbelief.

~The Weakness of the Flesh

It is written, *"Watch and pray, that ye enter not into temptation: the spirit indeed is willing, but the flesh is weak."* **(Mathew 26:41).** For the most part most of us are weak in the flesh. As long as you are weak in the flesh, you will not be able to pray.

It is written, *"For they that are after the flesh do mind the things of the flesh; but they that are after the Spirit the things of the Spirit."* **(Romans8:5).**

The weakness of the flesh will hinder anyone from praying to God. *"For to be carnally minded is death; but to be spiritually minded is life and peace. Because the carnal mind is enmity against God: for it is not subject to the law of God, neither indeed can be. So then they that are in the flesh cannot please God."* **(Romans8:6-8).**

~We Lack the Spiritual Discipline to Pray

It takes spiritual discipline to develop the attitude to pray often. Most young Christians lack the discipline to pray unto God.

We may be saved, sanctified and Spirit-Filled, but without discipline we will never enjoy prayerful time with the Lord.

The Psalmist wrote, *"Delight yourself in the Lord; And He will give you the desires of your heart."* **(Psalms 37:4)**. No one of us will make it with God without spiritual discipline.

~Sin in Our Life

As long as there is sin in our life, we will forever be reluctant to pray.

It is written, *"But if we walk in the light, as he is in the light, we have fellowship one with another, and the blood of Jesus Christ his Son cleanseth us from all sin. If we say that we have no sin, we deceive ourselves, and the truth is not in us. If we confess our sins, he is faithful and just to forgive us our sins, and to cleanse us from all unrighteousness."* **(1John1:7-9)**.

John Bunyon said, *"Prayer will make a man cease from sin as sin will entice a man to cease from prayer."*

~Laziness

Prayer is not a cheap talk, it takes spiritual, physical, and emotional energy to pray. Prayer is a form of labor. We were told, *"Epaphras, who is one of you, a servant of Christ, saluteth you, always labouring fervently for you in prayers, that ye may stand perfect and complete in all the will of God."* **Col4:12**

It is written, *"I beseech you, brethren, for the Lord Jesus Christ's sake, and for the love of the Spirit, that you strive together with me in your prayers to God for me"* **(Romans 15:30)**. We must strive in prayer to God. Therefore, our lack of prayer is often the result of laziness.

We are exhorted, *"not slothful (lazy or sluggish) in business, fervent in spirit, serving the Lord"* **(Romans 12:11)**.

"That ye be not slothful (lazy or sluggish), but followers of them who through faith and patience inherit the promises" **(Hebrews 6:12)**.

As long as I'm concerned, prayer demands concentration, devotion, effort, resolve and persistence. It is God's will for us to discipline ourselves in seeking His face in prayers. Isaiah said, *"There is none that calleth upon Thy name that stirreth up himself to take hold of Thee"* **(Isaiah 64:7)**.

~Lack of Focus

In my opinion, distraction and lack of focus will make anyone not to pray. Jesus said, *"And Jesus said unto him, No man, having put his hand to the plough, and looking back, is fit for the kingdom of God."* **(Luke9:62).**

In my opinion nothing should take priority over time with the Lord Jesus. Martin Luther said, *"I have so much to do that I shall have to spend the first three hours in prayer."*

~We are Faint Hearted

Although we are instructed by the Holy Scripture, that whatsoever we desire when we pray, we should believe that we receive them and we shall have them.

It is natural for an average man/woman to faint, especially if you pray and do not see result. It is written, *"Hope deferred maketh the heart sick: but when the desire cometh, it is a tree of life."* **(Proverb13:12)**.

We Lack the Spirit of Prayer

Perhaps you have never experienced it in life, but there is a spirit of prayer. Whenever anyone lack this spirit, we become empty and void. It is this spirit that grants us utterance and the motivation to pray.

It is written *"Likewise the Spirit also helpeth our infirmities: for we know not what we should pray for as we ought: but the Spirit itself maketh intercession for us with groanings which cannot be uttered."* **(Romans8:26)**.

CHAPTER 1

What are the Keys to Effective Prayer

Although it takes discipline and diligence to develop an effective and efficient prayer life, prayer must be offered unto God in faith, hope and with a heart of expecting result. Everyone desire to pray effectively but how many of us truly want to do what it takes for our prayer to prevail.

It is written *"And as he prayed, the fashion of his countenance was altered, and his raiment was white and glistering."* **Luke9:29**.

If Jesus pray until the fashion of his countenance was altered, so we ought to do the same to get the same result.

What are the secrets to having an effective prayer life?

"Elijah was a man subject to like passions as we are, and he prayed earnestly that it might not rain and it rained not on the earth by the space three years and six months. And he prayed again, and the heaven gave rain, and the earth brought forth her fruit." **James5:17-18**.

If the man of God-Elijah, prayed effectively, anyone can do the same. It takes total surrender unto the will of God for anyone to develop and effective prayer life.

Remember, *"There are many devices in a man's heart; nevertheless the counsel of the Lord, that shall stand."*

It is written, *"Declaring the end from the beginning, and from ancient times the things that are not yet done, saying, My counsel shall stand, and I will do all my pleasure."* **Isaiah 46:10**.

Chapter 1 - What are the Keys to Effective Prayer

The secret of effective prayer life is persistency, dedication, discipline, devotion, and diligence. Until you are consistent with your prayer life, you will not be productive and effective.

"Our prayers must be divinely directed." **(1 Kings 18:36)**.

Often Jesus will hear from the father before talking back to God.

As always Elijah heard from God and prayed accordingly. *"The word of the Lord came to Elijah"* **(1 Kings 18:1)**. And again, *"Let it be known, I have done all these things at thy word"* **(1 Kings 18:36)**.

Our primary prayer point must be divinely guided *"God how do you want me to pray?"* I'm convinced that if we would wait on divine direction from God, our prayer will be more effective.

We must pray in the name of Jesus Christ

Unless we pray in the name of Jesus you will not get result. For our prayer to be effective, it must be in the name of Jesus Christ.

"Wherefore God also hath highly exalted him, and given him a name which is above every name: That at the name of Jesus every knee should bow, of things in heaven, and things in earth, and things under the earth;" **Phi2:9-10**

We must pray according to His will

It is written *"For my thoughts are not your thoughts, neither are your ways my ways, saith the Lord. For as the heavens are higher than the earth, so are my ways higher than your ways, and my thoughts than your thoughts."* **Isaiah55:8-9**

The will of God is never our will. Unless we pray according to His will, our prayer will not yield much result.

Chapter 1 - What are the Keys to Effective Prayer

Jesus said *"After this manner therefore pray ye: Our Father which art in heaven, Hallowed be thy name. Thy kingdom come, Thy will be done in earth, as it is in heaven. Give us this day our daily bread. And forgive us our debts, as we forgive our debtors. And lead us not into temptation, but deliver us from evil: For thine is the kingdom, and the power, and the glory, for ever. Amen."* **Mathew 6:10-13**

We must pray for the revelation of God's glory

Every time we pray we must focus on the revelation of the glory of God. Whenever we pray in His name we must pray for revelation of God's glory. We must always examine our focus and define our purpose for praying for the revelation of God's glory.

It is written *"When the Lord shall build up Zion, he shall appear in his glory."* **Psalm 102:16**

We must pray in faith

Scriptures established clearly that without faith we cannot please God. For our prayers to work, we must understand the power of faith in prayer.

Jesus talking in the scriptures said, *"For verily I say unto you, That whosoever shall say unto this mountain, Be thou removed, and be thou cast into the sea; and shall not doubt in his heart, but shall believe that those things which he saith shall come to pass; he shall have whatsoever he saith."* **Mark11:23**

Use your imagination (John 5:17 and 19).

Visualize God doing what you're praying for and see it as completed. Jesus saw what the Father was doing in the spiritual realm before He did anything, and then acted accordingly. If we really believe something, our imagination will be stirred which will also stir our faith.

Chapter 1 - What are the Keys to Effective Prayer

Pray in the Spirit

Jude said, *"But you, beloved, building yourselves up on your most holy faith, praying in the Holy Spirit" (Jude 20). Paul said, "Praying always with all prayer and supplication in the Spirit, and watching thereunto with all perseverance and supplication for all saints"* **(Ephesians 6:18).**

Be bold when praying
(1 Kings 17:1, 18:44)

Elijah was bold in two ways:

He was confident in his declaration, and in what he believed God was going to do. Then he declared it.

He was bold in what he prayed for:

Elijah prayed that it wouldn't rain until he said it would. **(1 Kings 17:1).**

He prayed expecting life to come back into the widow's son. **(1 Kings 17:19-22).**

There had been a drought for three and a half years. Elijah dared believe God would make it rain again.

If we are afraid to exercise boldness in our prayer life, we will never experience great effects from our prayers. Psalms 81:10 says, *"Open thy mouth wide and I will fill it."* George Mueller said this meant we should *"open our mouth wide in big requests."*

Pray Specifically

The truth of the matter is, For unless we are specific in prayer we will not get the desired result. Jabez was very specific in his prayer request.

"And Jabez called on the God of Israel, saying, Oh that thou wouldest bless me indeed, and enlarge my coast, and that thine hand might be with me, and that thou wouldest keep me from evil, that it may not grieve me! And God granted him that which he requested." **1chronicle4:9**

Chapter 1 - What are the Keys to Effective Prayer

The blind Bartimaeus, the son of Timaeus, who sat by the highway side begging was very specific in his prayer request from Jesus Christ.

"And Jesus answered and said unto him, What wilt thou that I should do unto thee? The blind man said unto him, Lord, that I might receive my sight." **Mark 10:51**

Pray fervently (James 5:16-18).

Fervent means to *"work hard at, hot, boiling over, to put all you have into your praying."* If you are ever in a really desperate place and need someone's help, you won't calmly say to them, *"Would you mind helping me for a minute?"* No, you'd raise your voice (scream) and say, *"Help me now!"*

The early church prayed fervently for Peter and God sent an angel and miraculously delivered him out of jail and from the hand of Herod **(Acts 12:1-17)**.

It was said of Jesus, *"Who in the days of His flesh, when he had offered up prayers and supplication with strong crying and tears unto Him that was able to save Him from death, and was heard in that He feared"* **(Hebrews 5:7)**.

God told Isaiah, *"Put me in remembrance; let us argue our case together; state your cause that you may be proved right"* **(Isaiah 43:26)**. Let's remind God of His Word and put all we have into our praying.

Be persistent
(1 Kings 17:19-21, 18:41-44).

Whatever we praying for you must not loose heart and give up. True faith believes when we have prayed, we have already received what we have asked for **(Mark 11:22-24)** and goes on to continue to ask and remind God of our request until the answer to our request has materialized.

Scriptural examples of persistence in prayer:

The widow's son **(1 Kings 17:19-21)**.

Elijah praying for rain **(1 Kings 18:41-44).**

The Syrophonician woman **(Mark 7:24-30)**.

Jacob **(Genesis 32).**

A friend asking for bread at midnight **(Luke 11:5-10).**

The widow and the unjust judge **(Luke 18:1-8).**

Pray with anticipation **(1 Kings 18:41-45).**

When Elijah began to pray for it to rain again, after being dry for three and a half years, he prayed with expectancy. He put his head between his legs and prayed. He then asked his servant if he saw anything.

He said, *"there is nothing"*. He did this seven times, until after the seventh time the servant said, I see a cloud about the size of a man's hand. When Elijah heard this, he knew the rain was on its way. Pray and keep praying in faith, looking for and expecting your answer, until it manifest itself.

Anyone praying must be righteous. (James 5:16).

Righteousness is the key to answered prayers. God does not hear the prayer of sinners. **(See John9:31)**

Sins blocks our prayers from being heard and answered **(Isaiah 59:1-2; Psalms 66:18)**. It's extremely important to understand we have absolutely no righteousness of our own **(Isaiah 64:6; Romans 3:23)**.

The only righteousness we will ever have is imputed righteousness (2 Corinthians 5:21). That is why we need Jesus. He is the substitution for our sins. The moment we put our faith in Jesus as our only hope of salvation and the one who paid the penalty for our sins, we are declared righteous by God.

Jesus' righteousness is put to our account and we are righteous in God's sight. He sees us just as if we had never sinned. From that point on you can pray effectively as a righteous man or woman.

We also should daily ask God to search our heart for anything that may not be right with Him and make it right by confessing it as sin **(1 John 1:9)**. This should be done at the beginning of our prayer time.

We should also ask God to show us anything that might be wrong between us and any other person. If there is anything, we should do our best to make things right with them as well. This assures there is nothing standing in the way of our praying effectively.

"Therefore if you bring your gift to the altar, and there remember that your brother has something against you, 24 leave your gift there before the altar, and go your way. First be reconciled to your brother, and then come and offer your gift" **(Matthew 5:23-24)**.

If anyone has done us wrong or offended us in anyway, we must forgive them. *"Whenever you stand praying, if you have anything against anyone, forgive him"* **(Mark 11:25)**.

"Moreover if your brother sins against you, go and tell him his fault between you and him alone. If he hears you, you have gained your brother" **(Matthew 18:15)**.

Few reasons why prayerlessness is sin:

Prayerlessness Does Those Around Us a Disservice – **1 Samuel 12:23**

Even in their rebellious state Samuel would have been doing them a disservice not to continue to pray for them. We, likewise, are doing those around us a disservice when we fail to pray for them. Today, like never before, people desperately need our prayers.

Paul urges that prayers should be made on behalf of all men, for kings and all who are in authority **(1 Timothy 2:1-2)**.

Are we praying for our leaders? We have no right to complain about our leaders if we have not been consistently praying for them.

What about your pastor? He needs your prayers. Pastors often fight major spiritual battles as your spiritual leader that few are aware of. They need your prayers. Make a commitment today to doing spiritual warfare for your church, your pastor and our leaders as a nation.

Prayerlessness is Disobedience

We are commanded to *"pray without ceasing"* **(1 Thessalonians 5:17)**. Also, *"Men ought always to pray, and not to faint"* **(Luke 18:1)**.

"But thou, when thou prayest, enter into thy closet, and when thou hast shut thy door, pray to thy Father which is in secret; and thy Father which seeth in secret shall reward thee openly." **(Matthew 6:6)**.

Chapter 1 - What are the Keys to Effective Prayer

Failure to pray is direct disobedience to the command and will of God. If you do have a consistent prayer life, you should be encouraged that you are obeying God's Word, will and plan for your life.

Prayerlessness Reveals Our Unwillingness to Let God Work in Our Life

It was said of Jesus, *"He withdrew from them (His disciples) about a stone's throw, and He knelt down and began to pray, saying, Father, if You are willing, remove this cup from Me; yet not My will, but Yours be done. Now an angel from heaven appeared to Him, strengthening Him. And being in agony He was praying very fervently; and His sweat became like drops of blood, falling down upon the ground"* **(Luke22:41-44).**

Jesus, in the flesh, did not want to go to the cross. He knew what it would be like. He would not only face the physical and emotional pain of the cross, but God's wrath and separation from the Father, with whom He had experienced fellowship with throughout eternity past.

He wrestled with God in fervent prayer and surrendered to His will. It's in prayer that we allow God to mess in our lives. It's in our personal prayer experience that we often wrestle with God, our will is broken, and we surrender to His will. Not to pray is a refusal to let the Holy Spirit work in our life.

When we have a consistent prayer life, we are constantly giving God the opportunity to work in our life. It's only then that true surrender takes place.

Prayerlessness is Negligence of a Divine Privilege Purchased at a Great Price

"Let us therefore come boldly unto the throne of grace, that we may obtain mercy, and find grace to help in time of need" **(Hebrews 4:16).**

"Therefore, brethren, since we have confidence to enter the holy place by the blood of Jesus, by a new and living way which He inaugurated for us through the veil, that is, His flesh, and since we have a great priest over the house of God, let us draw near with a sincere heart in full assurance of faith" **(Hebrews 10:19-22)**

Chapter 1 - What are the Keys to Effective Prayer

Are we neglecting this divine privilege purchased for us at Calvary? Sadly, far too many of God's people are guilty of being negligent of this great privilege. Isaiah cried out, *"And there is none that calleth upon Thy name, that stirreth up himself to take hold of Thee"* **(Isaiah 64:7)**.

When Jesus went to the cross, suffered and died, the veil of the temple was ripped in two. This signified there would never again be anything keeping man out of God's presence when we come to Him through Jesus. Not to spend regular time with God in prayer is to neglect this divine privilege purchased at such a great price.

When we consistently spend time with the Father in prayer, we are taking advantage of this great privilege of entering God's presence and experiencing a touch and glimpse of His glory. *"By Whom also we have access by faith into this grace wherein we stand, and rejoice in hope of the glory of God"* **(Romans 5:2)**. Let's lay hold of this precious privilege purchased for us on Calvary.

CHAPTER 2
WHAT ARE HINDRANCES TO PRAYER

"For from the first day that thou didst set thine heart to understand, and to chasten thyself before thy God, thy words were heard, and I am come for thy words."
Daniel 10:12

To have an effective prayer life we must remove all hindrances to our prayers. If our bank account is overdrawn, the first thing we do is try to find the accounting error and fix it. If our car won't start we take it to a mechanic to trouble-shoot the problem and then repair the car.

If a businessman discovers he's running a loss he does a thorough investigation to find the culprit and correct it. Even so, if our prayer life isn't being fruitful we must find the root cause and reverse it.

As we look at possible hindrances to prayer, we inevitably must deal with negatives. However, the reverse side to every negative is a positive. As we explore hindrances to prayer, let's deal with the negative, but not forget to focus on the alternate positive.

Hindrances to an effective and fruitful prayer life:

Having a Wrong Relationship with God

The Bible says, *"For if, when we were enemies, we were reconciled to God by the death of His Son, much more, being reconciled, we shall be saved by His life."* **(Romans 5:10)**.

Prior to coming to Christ we were at enmity with God. The first and primary hindrance we must clear up is our relationship with God. We do this by being *"reconciled to Him (God) through the death of His Son."* The moment we come to Jesus for forgiveness and reconciliation, we are no longer enemies but beloved children.

Chapter 2 - What are Hindrances to Prayer

The opposite of having a wrong relationship with God is maintaining a close and intimate relationship with Him. This is the first step in having a good and fruitful prayer life. Much of our prayer time should be consumed in communing with God. As we spend regular time in fellowship with the Lord, developing a right relationship with Him, we will begin to discover our prayer life being more and more effective.

Having Sin in Our Lives

Sin is a barrier to fellowship with God and a major hindrance in our prayer life. The Psalmist said, *"If I regard iniquity in my heart, The Lord will not hear me"* **(Psalms 66:18)**.

To regard is to esteem, care for and hold dear to our heart. It is not necessarily something we did or fell into once but something we cling to. It is something we are clinging to and won't let go of. It may or may not be something that is outwardly visible to others, but something of the heart.

Isaiah said, *"Behold, the LORD's hand is not shortened, That it cannot save; Nor His ear heavy, That it cannot hear. But your iniquities have separated you from your God; And your sins have hidden His face from you, So that He will not hear"* **(Isaiah 59:1-2)**.

Sin must be dealt with and taken to the cross. If we confess our sins, He is faithful and just to forgive us our sins and to cleanse us from all unrighteousness. **(1 John 1:9)**.

Looking on the positive side, *"If we walk in the light (of His exposure) as He is in the light, we have fellowship with one another, and the blood of Jesus Christ His Son cleanses us from all sin"* **(1 John 1:7)**.

Don't hide or cling to sin of any kind but immediately bring it before God, confessing it, and let the blood of Jesus cleanse you of all sin. We should continually be asking God to turn His search light on in our heart to expose any area where we may be falling short. This is consistent with maintaining a right relationship with God.

Chapter 2 - What are Hindrances to Prayer

Not Believing God

Do we really believe and expect God to intervene and answer our prayers. Faith is the primary key to answered prayer. Paul said, *"How then shall they call on Him in whom they have not believed."* **(Romans 10:14)**

James wrote concerning prayer, We must *"Ask in faith without any doubting, for the one who doubts is like the surf of the sea, driven and tossed by the wind. For that man ought not to expect that he will receive anything from the Lord, being a double-minded man, unstable in all his ways."* **(James 1:5-8)**.

Clearly unbelief is a major hindrance to prayer.

On the other hand, faith is a great asset to an effective prayer life. If unbelief is a hindrance then faith promotes powerful praying. Jesus said faith has the power to move mountains **(Mark 11:22-24)**. He said, *"All things you ask in prayer, believing, you will receive"* **(Matthew 21:22)**.

There is power in believing God. Let's spend time cultivating and building our faith so we can believe God for great things. Below are a few ways to build strong faith;

Pray in accord with His will
(1 John 5:14-15).

When we know we are praying in line with His will, we can have faith and confidence He will grant the petitions we desire of Him.

Study the Word
(Romans 10:17).

Spending time in the Word of God helps build and strengthen our faith. Read and study it.

Meditate on the Word
(Psalm 1:2-3 and Joshua 1:8).

We need more than a casual reading of the scripture. We must spend time not only reading the Word but meditating on it.

Chapter 2 - What are Hindrances to Prayer

This means we take a passage, verse or phrase and toss it over and over in our mind, letting it sink deep within our spirit. This will build and strengthen our faith.

Use your Imagination (John 5:17 and 19).

See God doing what you're praying for. See it as a done deal. Jesus saw what the Father was doing in the spiritual realm before He did anything and then acted accordingly. If we really believe something our imagination will be stirred and our imagination will stir our faith.

Pray in the Spirit.

Jude said, *"But you, beloved, building yourselves up on your most holy faith, praying in the Holy Spirit."* **(Jude 20).**

Having Idols in Your Life

God demands to be first in our life **(Matthew 6:33 and Exodus 20:3).**

We must not allow anything to take priority in our life above Him. If we do it is idolatry. The elders of Israel came to Ezekiel to inquire of God and God spoke to Ezekiel saying, *"Son of man, these men have set up idols in their hearts and put wicked stumbling blocks before their faces. Should I let them inquire of me at all."* **(Ezekiel 14:3)**

God would not even listen to their prayers because they had *"set up idols in their hearts."* In contrast, if we are putting God first in our life, our prayers will flow before the throne of grace unhindered.

Neglecting to Pray

James said, *"You have not, because you ask not."* **(James 4:2)**. Neglect is inevitably a great hindrance to prayer.

Someone will say, *"But God knows what I want without my asking. He will do what He wants anyway."* Of course He does, but God wants us to ask. Though God desires certain things for His children, He refuses to act until we ask.

Chapter 2 - What are Hindrances to Prayer

Isaiah cried, *"There is none that calls upon Thy name, that stirs up himself to take hold of Thee"* **(Isaiah 64:7)**.

The writer of Hebrews wrote, *"Let us therefore come boldly unto the throne of grace, that we may obtain mercy, and find grace to help in time of need"* **(Hebrews 4:16)**.

Let's spend time laying hold of God and telling Him what we need and desire **(Psalms 37:4-5)**

Wrong Motives

James wrote, *"You ask, and receive not, because you ask amiss, that you may consume it upon your lusts"* **(James 4:3)**.

We so often pray with wrong motives. We go to God in prayer thinking, *"I don't care what God desires as long as I get what I want."*

Prayer is about implementing God's will in the affairs of men **(Matthew 6:10 and 1 John 5:14-15)**.

It's for His purposes and His glory **(John 14:13-14)**. Let's make sure our motives are right when we seek Him in prayer. If we do, we will find our prayers unfettered.

Indifference to God's Word

When we moved to our present church location, I went to visit a young man who had missed a few services.

He began to complain that God wasn't answering his prayers. I asked if he had been spending time in God's Word. He said he hadn't. I quoted Proverbs 28:9, *"He who turns away his ear from listening to the law (Word), Even his prayer is an abomination."* Then I looked him in the eye and said, *"Case settled!"*

Spending time in the Word is the key to a powerful prayer life. Jesus said, *"If you maintain a living communion with Me and My words are at home in you, I command you to ask, at once, something for yourself, whatever your heart desires, and it will become yours"* **(John 15:7 – West Expanded Translation)**

Chapter 2 - What are Hindrances to Prayer

The Word is paramount to maintaining a living communion with the God, praying in accord with His will and maintaining an effective prayer life. *See also James 1:22-25; Hebrews 2:1-3; 1 Peter 2:2; Psalms 1:2-3; Joshua 1:8.*

Having an Unforgiving Spirit

Jesus said, *"Whenever you stand praying, forgive, if you have anything against anyone"* **(Mark 11:25)**.

If you harbor resentment and unforgiveness toward anyone or anything, including situations and even God, it will greatly hinder your prayer life. You may have been legitimately wronged, but we must forgive as God has forgiven us.

Paul wrote, *"Let all bitterness, and wrath, and anger, and clamour, and evil speaking, be put away from you, with all malice: And be ye kind one to another, tenderhearted, forgiving one another, even as God for Christ's sake hath forgiven you."* **(Ephesians 4:31-32)**.

A forgiving spirit is essential to a good prayer life. *See also Matthew 18:21-35; Colossians 3:13.*

Bitter relationship with friends and family

Jesus said, *"Therefore if you bring your gift to the altar, and there remember that your brother has something against you, leave your gift there before the altar, and go your way. First be reconciled to your brother, and then come and offer your gift"* **(Matthew 5:23-24)**.

Jesus was essentially saying, before you go to God in prayer, do your best to make things right with anyone who thinks you have wronged them in anyway. It doesn't mean they are necessarily right, but just if they think you have wronged them.

If so, do your best to make amends with them. It's up to them if they will accept your apology or not. You must simply make a sincere attempt before God and the rest is up to them.

Chapter 2 - What are Hindrances to Prayer

The opposite stands true

If someone has offended you, you must go to them and attempt to make things right. Jesus said, "If your brother sins against you, go and tell him his fault between you and him alone.

"If he hears you, you have gained your brother" **(Matthew 18:15)**.

Notice he said, *"If he hears you."* He may or may not listen to you. It is your responsibility to go to him nonetheless, with hopes they will reconcile with you. You must take care to go to them in the right way. You must not go to them in pride and arrogance, but in humility. As we try to be in right relationships with all we know, we will see our prayer life flourish.

Not Keeping Your Marriage Strong (1 Peter 3:1-7)

In addressing the relationship between a husband and wife, Peter ends by saying, *"That your prayers will not be hindered"* **(1 Peter 3:7)**.

The relationship of a married couple can be very powerful in the spiritual realm. It can also be a great hindrance if the relationship is not right. This is why the devil does all he can to come between a couple and make them at odds with one another.

This is also why it is imperative we do all we can to deepen our relationship with each other, fight for one another and quickly reconcile when ever there is strife or disagreement. This is true physically, emotionally, spiritually and even sexually. **(1 Corinthians 7:1-5)**.

Let's fight for our marriage relationships *"That your prayers will not be hindered"* **(1 Peter 3:7)** but flourish.

Stinginess in Our Giving

The wise man wrote, *"He who shuts his ear to the cry of the poor will also cry himself and not be answered"* **(Proverbs 21:13)**. There is something about generosity that touches the heart of God.

Chapter 2 - What are Hindrances to Prayer

No, we can't buy the favor of God, but liberality in our giving and attitude reveals something about our heart. When we give liberally, with a right attitude, it releases the power and generosity of God in every aspect of life. We reap what we have sown.

Diligently study *Malachi 3:8-12; Luke 6:36-38; 2 Corinthians 9:6-10; 2 Corinthians 9:11-15; Galatians 6:6-10; 1 John 3:16-22.*

Satanic Resistance

We are in a constant struggle with the powers of darkness **(Ephesians 6:10-12)**.

They will fight us every step of the way. Daniel had been fasting and praying for twenty-one days when an angel appeared to him saying, *"Do not be afraid, Daniel, for from the first day that you set your heart on understanding this and on humbling yourself before your God, your words were heard, and I have come in response to your words.*

But the prince of the kingdom of Persia was withstanding me for twenty-one days; then behold, Michael, one of the chief princes, came to help me, for I had been left there with the kings of Persia" **(Daniel 10:12-13)**.

There was a spiritual battle raging from the time he first began praying. The devil hates praying people.

This is why we must engage in spiritual warfare. Prayer is more than just asking and receiving, it is a spiritual battle.

We must bind the strong man and all that stands against us **(Mark 3:27, Matthew 16:19, 18:18-20)**; join in agreement with other believers **(Matthew 18:18-20, Acts 4:23-24, 12:5; 12:12)**; pray in the spirit **(1 Corinthians 14:2)**; persist in prayer **(Genesis 32; Luke 18:1-8; Daniel 10:12-13)**; and yes, even fast as Daniel did if we are to gain ground in prayer.

Chapter 2 - What are Hindrances to Prayer

Let's not sit back casually letting the devil attack us but aggressively fight in prayer until we have been triumphant over every foe.

"From the days of John the Baptist until now the kingdom of heaven suffers violence, and violent men take it by force **(Matthew 11:12)**.

Prayer: Lord Jesus, we humbly come before You asking You to remove all hindrances to us having a productive prayer life. Please forgive us for the hindrances we have allowed to come into our life. We commit to prayer afresh and anew. Increase our faith so we can *once again believe You for great things. In Jesus name we pray, Amen!*

Every Christian should desire to be more like Jesus. One of the most effective ways to be more like Him is to emulate His prayer life. *"He that says he abides in Him ought himself also so to walk, even as He walked"* **(1 John 2:6)**.

"Therefore be imitators of God, as beloved children" **(Ephesians 5:1)**.

JESUS STYLE OF PRAYER

He prayed early in the morning. *"And in the morning, rising up a great while before day, He went out and departed into a solitary place, and there prayed"* **(Mark 1:35)**.

Jesus put the Father first, rising early in the morning to spend time with Him and so must we. We must give Him the first of our day before we do anything else.

Jesus rose early in the morning to seek the face of God. If we are to emulate Jesus we also must begin our day with prayer. Joshua began his day seeking God and as a result won the battle against Jericho **(Joshua 3:1 and 5:13-15)**.

We must seek the face of God first thing before the day's battle begins. Jesus knew this and that's why He rose early to pray before the day's battle began. We too must rise early to pray following Jesus' example.

Chapter 2 - What are Hindrances to Prayer

He prayed in a solitary. Jesus *"departed into a solitary place, and there prayed"* (**Mark 1:35**). There are times to pray publicly, but we need regular times alone with God as well.

Jesus said, *"But thou, when thou prayest, enter into thy closet, and when thou hast shut thy door, pray to thy Father which is in secret; and thy Father which seeth in secret shall reward thee openly"* (**Matthew 6:6**).

Jesus knew to have quality time with the Father He had to be completely alone where there would be no interruptions or distractions. It's in the solitary place that our relationship with God is developed. I find in the early hours of the morning my time with God is less likely to be interrupted.

If we are to pray like Jesus prayed, we must have a daily time of solitude where we are not distracted by phones, computers or anything else.

He prayed fervently. *"Who in the days of his flesh, when he had offered up prayers and supplications with strong crying and tears unto him that was able to save him from death, and was heard in that he feared"* (**Hebrews 5:7**).

He put His entire self (emotionally, spiritually, mentally and His flesh) into His praying. He prayed until He was exhausted and had to have an angel come to strengthen Him (**Luke 22:43**). It's usually in times of great distress that we pray the most fervently. Jesus was no different.

When facing the greatest battle of His life it was said of Him, *"And being in agony He was prayed the more fervently"* (**Luke 22:44**).

The early church emulated this facing threats for preaching the gospel, *"They lifted their voices to God with one accord"* (**Acts 4:24**).

When facing trouble with Peter's arrest, *"Peter was kept in the prison, but prayer for him was being made fervently by the church to God"* (**Acts 12:5**).

Chapter 2 - What are Hindrances to Prayer

If we are going to imitate Jesus' prayer life we must put everything we have into our praying.

Jesus prayed with dependency upon the Holy Spirit. *"The Spirit also helps our weakness; for we do not know how to pray as we should, but the Spirit Himself intercedes for us with groanings too deep for words"* **(Romans 8:26)**.

Jesus always prayed with dependency upon God's Spirit and we are instructed to do the same. We cannot pray adequately on our own. Jesus said, *"Apart from Me you can do nothing"* **(John 15:5)**. We too must pray with complete dependency upon the Spirit of God. See How to Pray in the Spirit.

He prayed in accordance with God's will. Jesus, being God in the flesh, knew the mind and will of God perfectly and always prayed accordingly. If we are to pray like Jesus we must pray according to God's will. In so doing we are assured of having our request heard.

John wrote, *"And this is the confidence that we have in Him, that, if we ask any thing according to His will, He heareth us: And if we know that He hear us, whatsoever we ask, we know that we have the petitions that we desired of Him."* **(1 John 5:14-15)**.

The only way we can be sure we are praying in God's will is to pray the Word of God – His revealed will. We must diligently study the Word of God to know how to pray in accord with His will **(2 Timothy 2:15)**.

It's a good practice to find scripture that pertains to your situation and begin praying the Word of God over it. We can never go wrong using the Word — in so doing, we can be assured we are praying as Jesus prayed.

He prayed in faith. Jesus said, *"All things, whatsoever ye shall ask in prayer, believing, ye shall receive"* **(Matthew 21:22)**.

Chapter 2 - What are Hindrances to Prayer

Again He said, *"Have faith in God. For verily I say unto you, That whosoever shall say unto this mountain, Be thou removed, and be thou cast into the sea; and shall not doubt in his heart, but shall believe that those things which he saith shall come to pass; he shall have whatsoever he saith. Therefore I say unto you, What things soever ye desire, when ye pray, believe that ye receive them, and ye shall have them"* **(Mark 11:22-24)**.

Jesus always prayed in faith, knowing God heard and would grant His request. When we pray according to God's will (as revealed through His Word) we can pray with faith knowing God desires to answer our prayers.

We are to put God in remembrance of His Word **(Isaiah 43:26)** and we can come into agreement with the Word of God in prayer **(Matthew 18:19)**, knowing He magnifies His Word above His name **(Psalm 138:2)**.

He visualized God answering His prayer. Jesus said, *"Truly, truly, I say to you, the Son can do nothing of Himself, unless it is something He sees the Father doing"* **(John 5:19).**

Before Jesus acted or prayed He visualized the Father doing it in the spiritual realm. As a result, it materialized in the natural realm. Likewise, we must see God doing the very thing we are asking of Him, which also stimulates our faith.

Jesus prayed with persistence. It was said of Jesus that He "prayed the third time, saying the same words" (Matthew 26:44). Jesus prayed the same thing multiple times. He was persistent in His praying. We are not to use vain repetition, however, there is a difference between repetition and vain repetition.

We can vocalize meaningless words in our prayers and people often do (like the Pharisees). There is also meaningful repetition like Jesus prayed.

Chapter 2 - What are Hindrances to Prayer

He prayed persistently the same thing until He had the breakthrough He needed and desired. We see persistent praying taught and exemplified throughout scripture.

Elijah stretched himself out over the widow's son three times until his life returned to him **(1 Kings 17:19-21)**; Elijah prayed for rain and had his servant look for a sign of rain seven times **(1 Kings 18:41-44)**; The Syrophonician woman kept crying out to Jesus **(Mark 7:24-30)**; Jacob wrestled with God until He blessed him **(Genesis 32)**; A friend asking for bread at midnight **(Luke 11:5-10)**; And the widow and the unjust judge **(Luke18:1-8)**.

Let's lay hold of God in persistent prayer and not let anything deter us until we've received what we are requesting of God **(Isaiah 64:7)**. In so doing, we will be emulating Jesus' prayer life.

CONCLUSION

"Therefore I say unto you, What things soever ye desire, when ye pray, believe that ye receive them, and ye shall have them." **Mark11:24**

We must all come unto repentance if we must encounter our savior Jesus Christ. Repentance is the key to deliverance, protection, and promotion.

"Therefore if any man be in Christ, he is a new creature: old things are passed away; behold, all things are become new." **2cor5:17**

Chapter 2 - What are Hindrances to Prayer

What must I do to determine my divine visitation?

To determine divine visitation you must be born again. The word says as many as received him, to them gave He power to become the sons of God. Even to them that believe on his name.

To qualify for divine visitation do the following sincerely;

1) Acknowledge that you are a sinner and that He died for you. **Rom3:23**.

2) Repent of your sins. **Acts 3:19, Luke13:5, 2Peter3:9**

3) Believe in your heart that Jesus died for your sin. **Romans10:10**

4) Confess Jesus as the Lord over your life. **Romans10:10, Acts2:21**

Now repeat this Prayer after me

Say Lord Jesus, I accept you today, as my Lord and my savior, forgive me of my sins wash me with your blood. Right now, I believe, I am sanctified, I am save, I am free, I am free from the Power of sin to serve the Lord Jesus. Thank you Lord for saving me. Amen.

Congratulations: YOU ARE NOW A BORN AGAIN CHRISTAIN

I adjure you to watch the Spirit of God bear witness with your Spirit confirming His word with signs following. The word says The Spirit itself beareth witness with our spirit, that we are the children of God. Join a bible believing church or join us on our weekly and Sunday worship services at 343 Sanford Avenue Newark New Jersey 07106.

Chapter 2 - What are Hindrances to Prayer

WISDOM KEYS

Every Productive Society is a society heading to the top

Millions of Nigerians run away from Nigeria, very few Nigerians stay in Nigeria.

My decision to return Nigeria is the will of God for my life

My short coming in America after 18 years, trained me to be wise, to think, reflect and reason appropriately.

If you train your mind to reason it will train your hands to earn money.

It is absurd to use the money of the heathen to build the kingdom of the living God.

Every Ministry reveals its agenda and goal either at the beginning or at the end. Be careful of your life it is your first Ministry.

The average American mind is conditioned for a continual quest to get new things and (discard the former) and throw away old things.

When I considered well, my BMW jeep became my initial deposit for the work of the ministry in Nigeria

Everyone is waiting for you to change your mind until you change your thinking nothing changes around you.

Multiple academic degrees in other discipline gave me the chance to think, reflect and reason

What so everyone are thinking and reflecting at the moment reveals you to the time and the now factor

All events and intents are the product of precise thought processes, accurate reason every event is designed for a designated timeline

Wisdom is your ability to think, to create and invent. If you can think wise enough you will come out of penury

The distance between you and success is your creative ability to think reason and reflect accurate.

Chapter 2 - What are Hindrances to Prayer

Success is the result of hard work, commitment resolve and determination learning from past mistakes and failing.

If you organize your mind you have organized your life and destiny.

There is a thin line between success and failure. If you look above and beyond you are on your way to success.

Wealth is your ability to think, power is your ability to reason and success is your ability to be informed.

If you can make use of your mind by thinking and reasoning God will make use of your life and destiny.

Think and Be Great

Reflect, Reason, think and be great

Famous people are born of woman

That you will make it is your intention; that you will survive is your resolve, that you will succeed with changes is your determination, personal efforts and hard work.

No man was born a failure. Lack of vision is the end product of failure.

Working with mental patients encourages and aspire me to be a productive observant and dedicated to my assignment.

Successful people are not magicians, it is the will power combined with hard work, and determination and a resolve to succeed that make them succeed.

In the unequivocal state of the mind, intention is not a location or a position it is the state of the mind.

So many people think that they think. The mind is used to think reflect and reason. You will remain blind with your eye open until you can see with your mind by thinking.

There is no favoritism in accurate and precise calculation

Chapter 2 - What are Hindrances to Prayer

Although knowledge is power, information is the key and gateway to a great future.

It will take the hand of God to move the hand of man.

With the backing of the great wise God, nothing will disconnect you from your inheritance.

As long as you have wisdom and understanding of God, Satan and evil cannot manipulate your life and destiny.

You have come this far by yourself judgment and decision you have made in the past, now lean and listen to God for another dimension of greatness.

Great people are common people it is extra ordinary effort and the price of sacrifice that produces greatness.

As a mental direct care worker I saw a great pastor and a motivational speaker within myself.

Menial job does not reduce your self-worth, until you resolve to achieve greatness see greatness in all you do; you will never count in your community

The principle of Jesus will solve your gambling and addiction problems

The man of Jesus will lead you into heaven,

Everyone have their self-appraisal and what they think about you. Until you discover yourself other opinion about you will alter the real you.

Supervisors and directors are just a position in the chain of command in a work place. Never allow your supervisor hierarchy to alter your opinion about yourself.

Everyone can come out of debt if they make up their mind.

That I am not a decision maker at work does not diminish my contribution to my world.

Although it appears like it was a poor decision to accept a direct care employment at a psychiatric hospital as I reflect of my nine years of experience, it became apparent that I have learnt and experienced enough for my next assignment.

Self-encouragement and determination is a resolve of the heart.

Chapter 2 - What are Hindrances to Prayer

If you are determined to make a difference, and do the things that make a difference you will eventually make a difference.

Good things do not come easy

Short cuts will cut your life short.

Those who look ahead move ahead.

Life is all about making an impact. In your life time strive to make an impact in your community.

Make friends and connect with people who are moving ahead of you in life.

If you can look around well you have come a long way in your life, made a lot of difference and realized a lot of success in life.

If you are my old friend, hurry up to reach out to me before I become a stranger to you.

Everything I am blessed with inspirations from God, that change my definition and interpretation of the world around me.

I thought I was stagnant and lonely until I looked around and noticed my children running around and my wife cooking.

At 40 I resigned my Job to seek the Lord forever.

My ministry took a drastic rise to the top when the wisdom of God visited me with knowledge and understanding.

You will be a better person if you understand the characteristics of your personality – your mood swings attitudes and habits.

It is the seed of love you sow into the heart of a child and a woman that you reap in due time.

Love is not selfish, love share everything including the concealed secrets of the mind.

As long as you have a prayer life and a bible; you will never feel lonely, rejected and idle in the race of life.

When good friends disconnect from you, let them go, they might have seen something new in a different direction.

Confidence in yourself and in God is the only way to bring you out of captivity

Never train a child to waste his/her time.

The mind is the greatest assets of a great future.

Chapter 2 - What are Hindrances to Prayer

You walk by common sense run by principles and fly by instruction.

Those who fly in flight of life fly alone.

Up in the air you are alone. No one can toll you accept the compass of knowledge and information

I have seen a tolling vehicle I have seen a tolling ship I have never seen a tolling airplane.

I exercise my judgment and make a decision every minute of the day.

Decisions are crucial, critical and vital with reference to your future.

So many people wish for a great future. You can only work towards a great future.

Your celebrity status began when you discovered your talent. What are you good at? Work at it with all commitment.

Prayers will sustain you but the wisdom of God will prosper you.

When I met Oyedepo, his teachings changed my perspective, but when I met Ibiyeomie; His teaching changed my perception.

I will be successful in ministry if only I concentrate and focus my energy in the work of the ministry.

It took the late Dr. Vincent Pearle Norman's book to open my mind towards kingdom success.

CHAPTER 3

PRAYER OF SALVATION

"Neither is there salvation in any other: for there is none other name under heaven given among men, whereby we must be saved." **Acts4:12.**

What must I do to determine my salvation?

To be saved we must be born again! The word says as many as received him, to them gave He power to become the sons of God. Even to them that believe on his name.

To qualify for divine visitation do the following sincerely,

1) Acknowledge that you are a sinner and that He died for you. **Rom3:23.**

2) Repent of your sins. **Acts 3:19, Luke13:5, 2Peter3:9**

3) Believe in your heart that Jesus died for your sin. **Romans10:10**

4) Confess Jesus as the Lord over your life. **Romans10:10, Acts2:21**

Now repeat this Prayer after me

Say Lord Jesus, I accept you today, as my Lord and my savior, forgive me of my sins wash me with your blood. Right now, I believe, I am sanctified, I am save, I am free, I am free from the Power of sin to serve the Lord Jesus. Thank you Lord for saving me. Amen.

I adjure you to watch the Spirit of God bear witness with your Spirit confirming His word with signs following. The word says The Spirit itself beareth witness with our spirit, that we are the children of God.

Chapter 3 - Prayer of Salvation

MIRACLE CARE OUTREACH

"...But that the members should have the same care one for another" **1cor12:25**

We are all members of the body of Christ. Jesus commanded us to love our neighbor as ourselves. This includes caring for one another as a member of one body. True love is expressed in caring and giving. The word says for God so Love He gave….

Reach out to someone in need of Jesus, help someone in crisis find Christ. Look out and prove your love to Jesus by caring and inviting your friends and associates to find Jesus the Healer.

Invite your friends to our Home Care Cell Fellowship (Miracle chapel Intl Satellite fellowship) In the USA at 33 Schley Street Newark New Jersey 07112.

If you are in Nigeria—**MIRACLE OF GOD MINISTRIES**

A.K.A "MIRACLE CHAPEL INTL"
Mpama –Egbu-Owerri Imo state Nigeria.

(Home Care Cell fellowship Group). We meet every Tuesday at 6:00pm-7:00pm.

LIFE IS NOT ALL ABOUT DURATION BUT ITS ALL ABOUT DONATION

What does the above statement mean?....

"Life consists not in accumulation of material wealth.." **Luke 12:15.**

"But it's all about liberality....meaning- what you can give and share with others." **Proverb 11:25.**

When you live for others--You live forever- because you out live your generation by the legacy you live behind after you depart into glory to be with the Lord. But when you live to yourself - you are reduced to self—you are easily forgotten when you die and depart in glory.

Permit me to admonish you today to live your life to be a blessing to a soul connected to you today.

Chapter 3 - Prayer of Salvation

I want you to know that so many souls are connected and looking up to you, and through you so many souls will be saved and rescued from destruction. Will you disciple someone today to find Jesus Christ?

"As a genuine Christian; it is your duty to evangelize Jesus Christ to all you meet on your way. Jesus is still in the healing business-Jesus is still doing miracles from time of old to now.

Therefore tell someone about Jesus Christ today, disciple and bring them to Church."

John 1:45 Philip findeth Nathanael....

Please to prove the sincerity of your love for God today; please become a soul winner. The dignity of your Christianity is hidden in your boldness to proclaim and evangelize Jesus Christ to all you meet on your way.

There is a question mark on the integrity of your Christianity until you become a life soul winner. Invite someone to join us worship the Lord Jesus this coming Sunday.

MIRACLE OF GOD MINISTRIES

PILLARS OF THE COMMISSION

We Believe Preach and Practice the following,

1) We believe and preach Salvation to every living human being

2) We believe and preach Repentance and forgiveness of sins

3) We believe and preach the baptism of the Holy Spirit and Spiritual gifts

4) We believe and teach the Prosperity

5) We believe and preach Divine Healing and Miracles (Signs &Wonder)

6) We believe and preach Faith

7) We believe and Proclaim the Power of God (Supernatural)

8) We believe and Proclaim Praise& Worship to God

9) We believe and preach Wisdom

10) We believe and preach Holiness (Consecration)

11) We believe and preach Vision

12) We believe and teach the Word of God

13) We believe and teach Success

14) We believe and practice Prayer

15) We believe and teach Deliverance

This 15 stones form the Pillars of Our Commission.

Become part of this church family and follow this great move of God.

MY HEART FELT PRAYER FOR YOU

It is my prayer that you testify today about the goodness of the Lord. I desire for you to have an encounter with our Lord Jesus Christ.

Now let me Pray for you:

Lord Jesus give this precious one reading this material heavenly vision that will give them purpose to live the remaining days of their lives. Lord God of heaven open a new chapter in the life of this precious love one reading this book today. May all their prayers be answered in the mighty name of Jesus. We thank you Jesus for hearing us. In Jesus mighty name. Amen.

CHAPTER 4
ABOUT THE AUTHOR

Rev Franklin N Abazie is the founding and Presiding Pastor of Miracle of God Ministries with headquarters in Newark, New Jersey USA and a branch church in Owerri- Imo State Nigeria. He is following the footsteps of one of his mentors, Oral Roberts (Healing Evangelist) of the blessed memory.

The Lord passed Oral Roberts healing mantle two days before he went to be with the Lord at age 91 into the hand of healing evangelist-Rev Franklin N Abazie in a vision.

In all his services the Power and Presence of God is present to heal all in his audience. He is an ordained man of God with a Healing Ministry reviving the healing and miracle ministry of Jesus Christ of Nazareth.

Pastor Franklin N Abazie, is called by God with a unique mandate:

"THE MOMENT IS DUE TO IMPACT YOUR WORLD THROUGH THE REVIVAL OF THE HEALING & MIRACLE MINISTRY OF JESUS CHRIST OF NAZARETH.

I AM SENDING YOU TO RESTORE HEALTH UNTO THEE AND I WILL HEAL THEE OF THY WOUNDS. SAID THE LORD OF HOST"

He is a gifted ardent Teacher of the word of God who operates also in the office of a Prophet, generating and attracting undeniable signs & wonders, special miracles and healings, with apostolic fireworks of the Holy Ghost.

He is the founding and presiding senior Pastor of this fast growing Healing ministry.

Chapter 4 - About the Author

He has written over 86 inspirational, healing and transforming books covering almost all aspect of divine healing and life. He is happily married and blessed with children.

BOOKS BY REV FRANKLIN N ABAZIE

1) Commanding Abundance
2) The outcome of faith
3) Understanding the secret of prevailing prayers
4) Understanding the secret of the man God uses
5) Activating my due Season
6) Overcoming Divine Verdicts
7) The Outcome of Divine Wisdom
8) Understanding God's Restoration Mandate
9) Walking in the Victory and Authority of the truth
10) Gods Covenant Exemption
11) Destiny Restoration Pillars
12) Provoking Acceptable Praise
13) Understanding Divine Judgment
14) Activating Angelic Re-enforcement
15) Provoking Un-Merited Favor
16) The Benefits of the Speaking faith
17) Understanding Divine Arrangement

18) Understanding Divine Healing
19) The Mystery of Endurance
20) Obeying Divine Instructions
21) Understanding the Voice of God
22) Never give up on Hope
23) The prevailing Power of faith
24) Understanding Divine Prosperity
25) The Reward of Prayer
26) Covenant Keys to Answered Prayers
27) Activating the Forces of Vengeance
28) Put your faith to work
29) Where is your trust?
30) The Audacity of the Blood of Jesus
31) Redeeming Your Days
32) The force of Vision
33) Breaking the shackles of Family Curses
34) Wisdom for Marriage Stability
35) Overcoming prevailing challenges
36) The Prayer solution
37) The power of Prayer
38) The Effective Strategy of Prayer
39) The prayer that works
40) Walking in Forgiveness
41) The power of the grace of God

42) The Power of Persistence
43) Overcoming Divine verdicts
44) The audacity of the blood of Jesus.
45) The prevailing power of the blood of Jesus
46) The benefit of the speaking faith.
47) Fearless faith
48) Redeeming Your Days.
49) The Supernatural Power of Prophecy
50) The companionship of the Holy Spirit
51) Understanding Divine Judgement
52) Understanding Divine Prosperity
53) Dominating Controlling Forces
54) The winners Faith
55) Destiny Restoration Pillars
56) Developing Spiritual Muscles
57) Inexplicable faith
58) The lifestyle of Prayer
59) Developing a positive attitude in life.
60) The mystery of Divine supply
61) Encounter with the Power of God
62) Walking in love
63) Praying in the Spirit
64) How to provoke your testimony

65) Walking in the reality of the Anointing
66) The reality of new birth
67) The price of freedom
68) The Supernatural power of faith
69) The intellectual components of Redemption
70) Overcoming Fear
71) Overcoming Prevailing Challenges
72) My life & Ministry
73) The Mystery of Praise

MIRACLE OF GOD MINISTRIES

NIGERIA CRUSADE 2012

MIRACLE OF GOD MINISTRIES
NIGERIA CRUSADE 2012

MIRACLE OF GOD MINISTRIES

NIGERIA CRUSADE

2012

www.ingramcontent.com/pod-product-compliance
Lightning Source LLC
Chambersburg PA
CBHW020035120526
44588CB00031B/691